MW00679201

A Survival Guide for the Groom to Be
(or how not to let sex become a fond memory)

by
Maureen Moss

Design & Illustration by
Randy Galloway

Printed in the United States of America
Library of Congress Catalog Card Number
96-83737
ISBN 0-9651310-1-7

Moss, Maureen.
A Survival Guide for the Groom to Be
(or how *not* to let sex become a fond memory)

Book design & illustrations by Randy Galloway

Published by
Constant Concepts, Inc.
3640 N. 38th Street
Suite 202
Phoenix, Arizona 85018
1-800-572-6647

First Printing June 1996

Acknowledgments

A sincere thanks to Randy Galloway for his ability
to draw my sense of humor.

Thank you Beth Meyer for your faith in me always
and laughing in all of the appropriate places.
Thank you for all of your hard work
but most of all thank you for your friendship.

And, thank you Hal Green for your support
on this project.

Table of Contents

Table of Contents

Table of Contents

Table of Contents

What You've Got To Look Forward To

1. Meet the In-Laws
2. Shave Twice-a-Day
3. Look at Flowers...a lot!
4. Plan Your Guest List
5. Give Up Golf
6. Your Life Is Over!

Men, You Need Help!

Men, you need help!
Consider this book your life line from this day
forward until you say your I do's.

The months ahead are going to be pure hell for
you. You will be drilled about your family's history:
"I hear there's been five divorces in your family.
What guarantee do I have that my daughter will
not be the sixth?" or, "Is it true that your father's
sister filed bankruptcy? Just how much money *is*
your family going to contribute to this wedding?"

Your Life Is Over

You'll be schlepped to look at flowers during the NBA playoffs, to the photographer's on your only day off and asked which tuxedo and what color you want, only to be told you *can't* wear that color! You'll have to prove yourself to her father, you'll be told you can't wear those old jeans to Grandma Esther's house, to cut your hair, shave (again) and keep your feet off the coffee table.

Your life as you knew it is over.!

Sex Will Be A Fond Memory

Sex will become a fond memory because she's too stressed and too tired from planning this wedding (it's taking everything out of her). And God forbid you don't pick up your clothes, help with the cooking, be more sensitive and stop watching sports all the time!

DON'T YOU KNOW
THERE'S A WEDDING TO BE PLANNED!!

Buckle Your Seat Belts

She will be worrying about every detail of the wedding for at least one year and will expect no less from you. Oh, did I mention your future mother-in-law becoming an INTEGRAL part of your life?

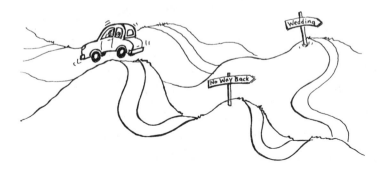

So buckle your seat belts because this is a trip you'd better be prepared for and I'm going to be your saving grace!

Digging Your Own Grave

Surviving planning a wedding and keeping your significant other in a "frisky" kind of mood is an art form. Compare it to mastering a juggling act – keeping your balls in the air at all times. If you can master this it will put you in the same league as Superman and Zorro. It will take macho to new and dizzying heights. It will prevent you from digging your own grave!

This Is Your Bible

Consider this book your "Bible" until you say your I do's. I am going to teach you not only successful survival techniques for the time that she and "her family" are planning "their" wedding (remember you and your family's input have little or no value at all), but also we will make sure that your bedroom does not pass for the local mortuary.

Men Are From Mars

Being a woman, I know what I am talking about guys – and being a woman who has planned thousands of weddings, the wisdom that I am about to impart on you – well, consider it a gift. We know that as Dr. John Gray says *Women are from Venus and Men are from Mars,* but any way you look at it, it's time to align the two species.

There are three things that a woman needs at this time in her life: Understanding, Romance and a charge card to Neiman Marcus.

How A Woman Thinks

What she doesn't need at this time is:

- To find your "little black book"
- To listen to you complain about her mother
- To find long hair on your jacket that doesn't match hers, the cat's or the dog

Once you men change your way of thinking, talking, eating and breathing, you will understand the way a woman thinks. As for Romance, 98% of you have about as much of a clue about that as to where the Loch Ness Monster *really* lives.

Those Three Little Words

Women like the "little" things in life too, like: *a little bouquet of flowers*, or *a cute little kitten or puppy*, or *a nice little card* that you can pick up at 7-11 (you're there anyway picking up a 12-pack), or *Three Little Words* — *I Love You*.

Grooms-to-be, I believe in you. You can count on me. While she's planning the wedding, we'll be planning your survival.

Chapter 1

Don't Drop Your Balls Now...

Guys, You Lucked Out!

Guys, you lucked out — you found the woman of your dreams and you've convinced her that you are her Prince Charming. Now, I'm sure that you put time, thought, and energy (not to mention a few bucks) into wooing her. I'm sure that you made some sacrifices (and you didn't wither and die from it). You probably missed a football or basketball game here and there to take her to a movie  or a concert. I'm sure you told her how beautiful she looked, that she smelled great, her skin was so soft and what a body!

You Shaved Before Sex

You were probably sexually innovative and unselfish. You probably gave her back rubs and even let her "*in*" where no woman has been allowed before. I'm sure you sent her flowers, helped with the dishes, took out the garbage, and supported her when she had a fight with her mother. You probably even brushed your teeth and shaved whenever possible before sex. (If you cannot relate to the above, stop now and return this book to your local bookstore– *you are hopeless!*)

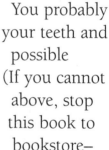

Big Night!

Consider The Alternatives

You Could Be:

1. Eating something you can't identify from a carton in the refrigerator.

2. Searching for the "other" sock that matches.

3. Figuring out why your white jockey shorts turned pink.

4. Having no one but yourself to blame for the dent in your car.

5. Sharing the sofa with an empty case of beer and an empty pizza box.

Consider The Alternatives

You Could Be:

6. Bowling on an all men's league.

7. Trying to analyze yourself.

8. Spending your weekend going through the "personal" ads.

9. Worse yet, you could be writing your own "personal" ad.

10. Watching the perfect sunset with your dog.

Now That She Has Accepted

So now that she has accepted your very sincere marriage proposal and believes that life will continue in such bliss, why have you started passing gas in public, throwing your jock strap on the floor (like she really wants to step on *that* thing), become a channel surfer passing right over her favorite TV shows, sit on the toilet with *Penthouse* for an hour, call her mother every horrible name in the English language as well as six other languages, leave hair in the sink when you're done shaving, send her "air flowers"(you know those invisible ones 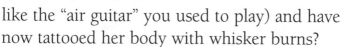 like the "air guitar" you used to play) and have now tattooed her body with whisker burns?

Show Your True Colors

Guys, you don't want to show your true colors now! Not when she's planning the most important day in your life. (That is what she told you, isn't it?) You must keep up your act and after awhile it will become a way of life.

When You Were A Kid

Let me relate to you on a guy's level, I'll compare this to sports; remember when you were a kid and you started playing baseball  (you may insert the sport of your choice), you could hardly even hit the ball. You couldn't run very fast, and it seemed at times that there was a hole in your mitt. You were frustrated because not only were you not a very good baseball player, but everyone else was frustrated too, your dad and your teammates. But you were determined to get good.

And It Paid Off

Baseball (or whatever) was very important to you. So you practiced, you put other things aside so you could practice and get good at it. You loved this game. You took advice from your coach and you found ways to get better. You invested time and it paid off. You hit your first home run and from there you got confident and you got better and better. You were happy, your coach was happy, your dad was happy and so were your teammates.

I knew he could do it!

BEST

Keep Hitting Home Runs

Well, grooms-to-be, that's how you need to approach your relationship with your bride-to-be, and I promise you will continue to hit home runs. You need to practice patience, you need to practice listening, you need to practice being the same charming guy that she fell in love with. You need to practice getting up in the morning and while you are brushing your teeth think of one thing you can do or say to her that will make her happy. (It's a proven fact that man can brush and think all at the same time.) You need to continue asking her out on dates, continue making love in new and unusual places, continue letting her fall in love with you. Don't change courses now. Don't be stupid, you had to do something right to get this far. This is not a science project — *it's common sense!*

Chapter 2

A Penny Saved Means Absolutely Nothing

Regarding Marriage If You Look At It This Way:

You will never feel alone again.	▶	You can now even sit on the toilet and have a meaningful conversation.
You will never be cold in bed during those long winter nights.	▶	Her long flannel nightgown and wool socks will surely keep you warm.
You will never again have to search for the sports page from the morning paper.	▶	Since the new puppy is being paper trained you can now sit (comfortably) on the floor and read it.
You no longer have to exist on freezer food popped into the microwave for dinner.	▶	You will now be the "proving grounds" for every recipe from *The Joy of Cooking*.

Fork Up Some Dough

The first curve that's going to come to you when planning this wedding is how much money

If You Need Extra Money
Consider Calling:

- Your former college roommate •
- • Your bookie •
- • The guy you made friends with
the night of your DUI •

(do *not*—and I repeat *do not* hock anything
that she has given you as a gift!)

are you (and/or your family) going to come up with to help pay for this wedding.

Time To Pay Up

Now don't get crazy. This is important, and when she says she needs to know right now, she does. I know that you think that the bride is supposed to pay for everything, but there are some things that you are responsible for, such as the bride's bouquet (you see, we're back to that flower thing again),

the mothers' corsages, the boutonnieres for the groomsmen, the officiant's fee (that means minister, rabbi, etc.), the rehearsal dinner, the marriage license and the honeymoon.

He's Just A Bum

Also, if your family is inviting more guests than the bride's side of the family can afford, you need to be responsible for that too. Now, if you give her grief on this subject, this is what you can expect: her father will tell her she's marrying a cheapskate, her mother will shake her head and say, "I told you he was a bum," (not to mention your no-good parents) and she will begin to look at you with veiled eyes.

Is It Worth It?

So I ask you, "Is it worth it?" The intelligent thing to do is to invite your parents and her parents out to dinner to discuss this "delicate" matter and you pick up the tab. Now I guarantee you will not go to bed empty handed.

Restaurants I *Wouldn't* Suggest

- Taco Bell -
- Long John Silvers -
- Harvey's Wineburgers -
- Chucky Cheese Pizza -

Chapter 3

Bringing Patience To New And Dizzying Heights

A Matter Of Life & Death

If you are to survive this wedding planning process you must ALWAYS remember one thing: planning a wedding is only a teeny weeny bit simpler than planning the President's Inaugural Ball. So, if you look at it this way you will understand the continual need for immediate decisions that are a matter of life or death, the continual anxiety attacks, and the unbearable stress that she's under that leads to eating disorders, such as eating everything in the refrigerator at one sitting except for door food (you know, mustard, ketchup, mayonnaise, that kind of stuff).

The Joy of Sex

You will understand why your night stand (and hers), along with every bit of available counter-space, houses every bridal magazine from the United States to France as well as books on "Getting to Know the Man You Are Going to Marry," "Getting The Love You Want," "Keeping The Love You've Got" and "The Joy of Sex" (as if it weren't joyful before she got engaged).

Suggested reading for you:

► "Mars and Venus in the Bedroom"
by John Gray, Ph.D. ◄

Call Waiting and Waiting

You will understand why your friends can no longer call you on the phone because she's on the phone telling someone (anyone) about the wedding, while another one of her friends is on call waiting, patiently waiting to hear the same story.

You will gain tremendous knowledge from this wedding planning experience as well. You will have a clear understanding of the difference between white, off-white, ivory, eggshell and candlelight. You will come to understand the difference between cocktail length, tea length and floor length. You will learn that the true meaning of your nest egg is not for saving for a rainy day, but for "her" wedding day — and I'm sorry to tell you this men, but PMS has now joined forces with PWS (Pre-Wedding Syndrome) and lasts for 21 days in the month.

How Do You Survive

> ## Definition of PWS:
> Pre-Wedding Syndrome
> The stress, anxiety, uncertainty and
> intimidation that comes with
> planning a wedding.
> Warning: PWS is highly contagious, keep a
> close eye on your household pets.

So, how do you survive this? Simple. Just let her know how much you care about this wedding, too. (Act if you must, even if you would prefer to go to one of those drive-through chapels in Las Vegas.)

You Know You Can Trust Her

Let her know you trust her judgment on which color napkins to choose and it's okay if they don't exactly match the cummerbund of your tuxedo.

> *When shopping for your cummerbund,*
> *stay away from those*
> *that have football helmet designs*
> *on them.*

Chapter 4

You Are Responsible For
(You *"Are"* Responsible, "Aren't" You?)

GIFTS
GUESTS
PHOTOS
RING
HONEYMOON
REHEARSAL DINNER
BACHELOR PARTY

Your Little "To Do" List

Ask her to give you a list of what you can do to alleviate some of this "pressure." Since she doesn't entirely trust your judgment on events surrounding this critical day, the list will be short. I guarantee it. This is an overview of what you'll probably have to do (don't worry, I'll walk you through it):

- Gather your guest list
- Select the photographer
- Hire the band or DJ
- Learn to dance
- Decide who will marry you and what you will say
- Plan the Rehearsal Dinner
- Give tokens of your appreciation to groomsmen and ushers
- Plan the infamous Bachelor Party with your best man
- Get tuxedoes
- Plan the honeymoon
- Buy her a wedding present

Jump In With Both Feet

Now take a deep breath and jump in with both feet–

it won't kill you, just some minor discomfort!

How To Dig Your Own Grave
(Or how *not* to score)

1. Say "I told you so."

2. Hang up the phone on her.

3. Leave empty ice cube trays on the day of a party.

4. Tell her she's a lousy driver.

5. Walk away and say "you don't want to talk about it."

6. Tell her your old girlfriend would never have said that.

7. Leave the toilet seat up.

8. Tell her she's stupid.

9. Put the guys before her.

10. Criticize her family.

Chapter 5

Your Guest List
(Not The Entire Football Team Replete With Cheerleaders)

Your Guest List

Get your family's guest list together. Call your parents and tell them you need the names, addresses and phone numbers of everyone they want to invite to the wedding. Now write your list. Give the lists to the bride-to-be.

Those Friends of Yours

First mission accomplished – unless she starts complaining about:

(a) The fact that your family invited too many people and what do you think her family is, millionaires? or. . .

(b) She will not have those immature friends of yours at her wedding — every time they're in public they embarrass her.

> **Do Not Invite
> Any Old Girlfriends!!!!!**

In the event that this happens, just smile (remember the *enormous* pressure she is under) and tell her that you will talk to your parents about scaling down the list a bit, and that you will make your friends swear they will have no more than one drink per hour.

Have You Lost Weight

Then immediately ask her if she's lost weight (women love this) because she looks incredible today, and how about if you make dinner tonight? (What a man, major brownie points here!)

Chapter 6

A
Picture
Is
Worth...

Get Emotion Packed Photos

The next thing she will ask you to do is go with her to the photographer.

Making a decision as to which photographer to use is an important one. Good photography is emotion packed and will invoke loving emotions in both of you.

Splurge on Great Photos

It is important to make this decision together. Don't be impatient with her and don't rush your decision about which photographer to choose. You want to find the perfect photographer that will give you a wedding album full of memories. When you look back at those pictures years later, it won't matter that you almost had to file bankruptcy for all those "little extras" that she forgot to put in her parent's budget – or that you had to hang all your clothes from your walk-in closet in the hall closet because her wedding dress was in your closet and *nothing* could touch it because it might wrinkle.

Your Heart Will Melt

You'll look at her, looking at you in those pictures with eyes of love and your heart will melt. She'll look at you in those pictures and remember how tolerant you were of her when she took the entire right quarter panel off your new car backing out of the garage on her way to one of the eleven fittings for her wedding gown.

She'll also remember that you never once complained when she slept at her parents' house for one month straight before the wedding for good luck.

With Wedding Album Eyes

She'll look at you, looking at her in that wedding album with eyes full of love and understanding and fall in love with you all over again. Ah yes, a picture is worth a thousand words.

11. Leave wet towels on the bathroom floor.

12. Use the last sheet of toilet paper, and not replace it.

13. Come home with alcohol on your breath after a hard day's work.

14. Swear at her.

15. Hire an old girlfriend to work in your office.

16. Invite an old buddy to spend "a few days with you."

17. Tell her she's too sensitive.

18. Leave hair in the bathroom sink.

19. Remember your secretary's birthday, and not hers.

20. Stare at another woman when you're out with her.

21. Mention that she looks like she's put on a few pounds.

Chapter 7

Set The Night To Music– Band or DJ?

Pearl Jam Won't Work

Next on your list will be going together to listen to bands or DJ's for your big day. Take her out for a nice dinner first, check out the band or DJ, and then take her dancing afterwards. From your first step down the aisle, to your first step on the dance floor, the music will be key to setting the mood. Now grooms-to-be, you must understand that you cannot have the same band (or DJ) at your wedding that plays at the local nightclub (or the DJ that plays at your favorite strip club). The band or DJ you select must have a repertoire that consists of more than Pearl Jam, Metallica or cuts off of the Rolling Stones "Voodoo Lounge" album. Wedding music must be appealing to the young and old. It needs to be romantic at times, fun and upbeat at times and maybe even ethnic. Your grandparents will want to dance to it as well as your buddies.

Avoid The Drunk DJ

The traditional first dance is EXTREMELY important to her. Don't suggest "Love Hurts" for your first dance and don't have Rod Stewart singing "Oh Maggie I Wish I'd Never Seen Your Face." When you decide on your band (or DJ) make certain you let them know how you want them to dress; that they cannot drink while on the job (no matter how much fun you think it would be to party with them). Be sure that the people you've seen play are the exact people you have at your wedding. Get this, and all wedding arrangements in writing.

Additional songs NOT to suggest:

- "I Will Survive"
- "Hang On Sloopy"
- "Take Me to the River"
- "Desperado"

Dance Lessons ...No Way!

Looks like Grandma could use some catnip!

Now, let me warn you what could happen at this juncture. Your bride-to-be may decide it would be a great idea to take some dance lessons. (Don't cringe.) She's not suggesting you be Fred Astaire to her Ginger Rogers, she just doesn't want you to embarrass her since you will also be required to dance with her mother, your mother, your grandmother and the maid of honor. So what the heck guys - this could be fun - another challenge ... And the rewards, oh the rewards...

Just Sway Left & Right

Now, if you flat out refuse to take dance lessons do this: when you are dancing with your bride, hold her very, very close and just sway left to right, barely (and I mean barely) move your feet and turn (slowly) as you sway.

> The feelings of discomfort you are
> now experiencing will pass . . .
> *like gallstones.*

This is the best chance you have of not stepping on her feet. Gaze lovingly into her eyes and tell her how happy you are that she is your wife (she will love to be called "your wife" at this particular moment).

Now Talk A Lot

When you have to dance with everyone else, talk
a lot, comment on the food, the flowers, the valet
parking and how nice it is to see *Uncle Milton*
after all these years (never draw attention to the
music). Distraction is the key and before you
know it the dance is over.

How To
Score Points
(Or how to score)

1. Send her flowers at work for no particular reason.

2. Help her put her clothes on.

3. Book a day for her at the local spa for no particular reason.

4. Put an extra $20.00 in her wallet and don't tell her.

5. When you're wrong, admit it and apologize.

6. Hold her hand during a movie.

7. Massage her feet.

8. Take her car to the car wash.

9. Pick up the drycleaning.

10. Buy her that new CD she's been wanting.

How To
Score Points
(Or how to score)

11. You be the one to stop at the grocery store on the way home.

12. Ask her out on a date.

13. If you're going to be late, call her as soon as you know.

14. Buy her something, anything in her favorite color.

15. Bring home a stuffed animal for her.

16. Never go to bed angry.

17. Do nice things for no particular reason.

18. Give as much as you get.

19. Polish her toenails.

20. Flirt with her.

Chapter 8

I Now
Pronounce
You...

Live Together?!

Who Will Marry You

You will now go together to visit the person who is going to marry you. The priest or minister or rabbi you are going to meet with is the closest you are going to get to GOD, so don't mess up. Remember, they have their own set of rules (like God) and it is not for you to question why.

We Don't Have Time

If they tell you you have to go to pre-marital counseling, don't beg them to overlook this part of it because you just don't have time. Perhaps you could schedule your counseling sessions on the same night as your dance lessons (now, won't that be festive!).

Tips for Pre-Marital Counseling:
•
Do *not* discuss your sex life
•
Do *not* tell them you don't believe in God
•
Do *not* tell them how much you *really* drink
•
Do *not* tell them you tried marijuana
but didn't inhale

Here A Vow There A Vow

You will talk about your vows. I will tell you right now that a lot of women think it would be *soooooooooooooo* romantic if you both wrote some of your vows. (Don't cringe.)

Some Vows She Would Love to Hear

I vow to love you no matter how much weight you gain

I vow to call your mother once a week

I vow to stay up with you all night when our children are born

Hire A Ghost Writer

You have one of three choices. You can:

a) Go to the library where they have several books on writing your own vows and you can use these as a guideline, or

b) You can plagiarize, or

c) You can hire a ghost writer. The choice is yours.

Regarding Marriage

If You Look At It This Way:

You will no longer have to just stare at the road when you are driving your car. ▶	She will insist that you look at her when she is talking to you.
When you go to the movies there will no longer just be men in trench coats in the theatre. ▶	There will be lots of families with adorable little kids sitting right next to you.
You will never have to iron your own shirts again. ▶	The dry cleaner is happy to iron all of your shirts and send you the bill at the end of the month.

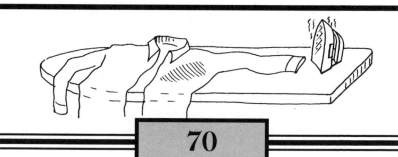

70

Chapter 9

The Tux

Your Tux Must Match

Selecting your tuxedos is next on your list. You may even get to do this on your own (or with your best man). Of course, if you are doing this on your own, rest assured you will be carrying a swatch of the bridesmaids' dress with you so you can match the color of the cummerbund and bowtie EXACTLY. (Listen, it could be worse, you could be schlepping the whole dress.)

Not The Neon Vest

If you are going alone you will also be given EXACT instructions from your bride-to-be on acceptable tuxedo styles, colors, color of shirts, to have vests or not to have vests, to have a solid or print vest, matching handkerchiefs (or not), shoe styles and colors, and whether the color of studs for your shirts should be black, silver or gold.

FYI:
When the formal wear merchant talks to you about "studs" to wear with your tuxedo - he (or she) is NOT referring to you and your friends - they are referring to button covers!

If you are not taking "accurate" notes, you may just want to take your bride-to-be with you. It will be easier, it will be another bonding experience.

Men, It's Only Fitting

Make sure that all of the men (and the ring bearer) get their tuxedos at the same shop. If some of your groomsmen are from out of town have them go to a local formal-wear merchant to have exact measurements taken and sent directly to you. You, in turn, will take them to your tuxedo shop. As soon as the groomsmen arrive in town have them go for a fitting of their tuxedos.

The good thing about guys being fitted for their tuxes in advance is that they don't have the *insane* idea (like some brides we know and love) that they will *definitely* be losing 35 pounds before the wedding (the fact that the wedding is only four weeks away doesn't matter – they *will* lose the weight!)

On The Look-Out

Be sure to find out when you have to have the tuxedos returned and assign someone (preferably your best man) to be responsible for getting them back. You don't want the tuxedo shop putting out an APB on you for tuxedo theft.

Dunk
And
You're
Shrunk

Also, if your reception is anywhere near water, have your groomsmen restrain themselves from throwing you in with your tux and shoes. It has been known to happen. Your rental will then have gone from $69.00 to $269.00 and where are you going to have the opportunity to wear a shrunken tuxedo?

Chapter 10

Ahh, Yes

THE Bachelor Party

The Need To Be Fools

Ah Yes - "THE" Bachelor Party
. . . . .Let me insert a little footnote here on the bachelor party. We women understand the need for you guys to go out and make complete fools of yourselves one more time before you enter what you have been told is indentured servitude. As a wedding consultant for 10 years, I've heard all of the stories from the brides about the infamous bachelor party that almost ended the marriage before it began.

A Cold Day In ...

I recently read a story (honest) about a bachelor party where the groom got so drunk he passed out. Then his "friends" loaded him into the cargo department of a plane going to Alaska (don't ask me how, I wasn't there) and when he woke up, it was the day of his wedding and he was in a different state and couldn't get back in time for the wedding. The bride then sued him for all of the financial loss to her family!

Don't Mess With Her

I swear, when you think about the number of opportunities a woman has to poison her man, it's amazing that it doesn't happen more often! Guys, you would be better off to play Truth or Dare with Sadam Hussein then mess with your bride at this late date.

Enough said.

Chapter 11

The Rehearsal Dinner

(Not To Be Held At Your Favorite Strip Club)

Regarding Marriage

If You Look At It This Way:

If you have any aches or pains you won't have to run to the store for aspirin.	In your very own medicine cabinet there will be: Midol, Tylenol, Valium, Maalox, Ex-Lax, Pepto Bismol, Preparation H, Ora-Gel, Tums, Prozak and Nair (in case you don't want to shave).
You won't have to pay the bills.	You won't be able to.
You will no longer have to figure out how to get in touch with your feelings.	The path will be paved for you.
You will no longer need to count calories and fat grams from big juicy cheeseburgers.	There are very few calories in Tofu and Bean Sprout sandwiches.

Not Pizza and Bowling

It is now going to be up to you and your family to plan the traditional rehearsal dinner. (Hang in there men, we're almost done). The traditional rehearsal dinner is always held immediately following the rehearsal for your wedding ceremony. Depending on the budget, you may have the dinner at home or at a restaurant. (This is a ripe opportunity for your parents to get in good with her parents). I don't recommend pizza and bowling.

Who's Comin' to Dinner

The dinner should include both immediate families, the wedding party, the officiant who is marrying you or anyone else that is extremely close to you. It is also a great opportunity to invite out of town guests.

At this dinner, be your most romantic, charming self to "their" daughter. This will also be the perfect opportunity to thank her parents for giving birth to the most incredible woman in the world! (How's that for schmoozing?!)

Regarding Marriage

If You Look At It This Way:

You no longer have to drink alone.

▶ It will now be much more fun to sit in a bar with your wife, then with a bunch of rowdy, sports-loving, girl-watching guys.

You never have to just sit at a football game and concentrate on the game.

▶ You are now able to get up at least once during each quarter and get nachos, Diet Pepsi, more ice, and escort her to the bathroom (and wait).

You will never again forget Mother's Day, Father's Day, birthdays (or any other days requiring a gift).

▶ There will be post-its on the bathroom mirror, in your brief-case and on the dashboard of your car, reminding you.

Giving The Gifts

At this dinner you will present your best man, your groomsmen and ushers with gifts as your token of appreciation for them standing up for you at the wedding.

GIFT IDEAS

Tickets to a Sporting Event

A Desk Clock

Personalized Beer Mugs

A Money Clip

A Nice Pen

Gifts From The Heart

YOU DO NOT WANT TO GIVE THE FOLLOWING GIFTS:

a) A subscription to "Playboy" magazine

b) A gift certificate to Sportsman's Liquor Barn

c) Paraphernalia from Zorbas House of Sex

d) A gift certificate for two table dancers at their *favorite* club

e) Backstage passes to the next Frederick's of Hollywood's lingerie show

Watch Your Every Move

Remember, her parents will still be watching your every move and if you are an embarrassment to the family you will hear about it for the next twenty or so years ... And, the officiant, who is the closest thing to GOD (remember) is taking notes and passing them on to a higher authority.

Don't Drink Too Much

Don't drink too much (you're probably still running on fumes from the bachelor party anyway) and don't go out bar hopping with the guys, just one more time, after the rehearsal dinner.

Restrain yourself, tomorrow is the Big Day!

The True Definition Of The Big Day

The Day When PWS (Pre-Wedding Syndrome) is Finally Over!

Regarding Marriage

If You Look At It This Way:

You won't have to settle for one of those table top Christmas trees that you picked up at the grocery store.	You can now go up north in 50 degree below zero weather to chop down a nice big one, strap it on the hood of your new BMW, and set it up in the living room where the TV used to be.
You will never have to own one of those small, sleek sportscars again.	You can now be the proud owner of a station wagon with wood panels on the door, lots of room for kids, dogs and groceries and a shiny new luggage rack on the hood.
You will be able to see your woman as you've never seen her before.	With green mask on her face, hot rollers, red blotches on her face after steaming her pores open, and cotton between her toes as her nails are drying.

Chapter 12

Last-
But
Certainly
Not
Least
(Trust Me)

THE
Honeymoon

Escape To Find Peace

Last, but certainly not least (trust me) is planning the honeymoon. Once you've survived the wedding plans and the big day itself, you'll feel like you need to either:

a) go to a VA hospital

b) be debriefed

c) go on a leisurely honeymoon and find the romance, without interruption, you had before *"The Wedding!"*

Just Bring A Bikini

I suggest the latter. Although it is your responsibility to pay for the honeymoon, it is imperative that you discuss the destination with the Mrs.-to-be. This is not the time to take a scene from a movie and tell her "it's a surprise, just pack summer things." She wants to know exactly where she's going so she can determine how many suitcases she has to pack and how many empty extra ones she needs to bring along for all that she's going to buy.

Not To The Cubs Game

I will tell you for sure where she won't want to go and spare you an argument:

a) wherever the Cubs are having spring training

b) anyplace you can contract Montezuma's revenge

c) anyplace you took an ex-girlfriend

d) anyplace that doesn't have a toilet indoors

e) anyplace that doesn't have an outlet for a
   blow dryer

f) anyplace that the American dollar is de-valued

g) anyplace that doesn't have a mall

h) wherever there's a sports bar in walking distance

Just For The Two Of You

Your honeymoon destination should have one main focus – romance, and lots of it. There are a few things that you should insist on (man that you are):

a) no bridal magazines allowed

b) she cannot write thank you notes on this trip

c) her parents cannot come along

Plan Your Trip Early

It is important that you plan your honeymoon far enough in advance so that you won't have to *"settle"* for anything. Believe it or not guys, in the back 25-50 pages of bridal magazines there are great in-depth ideas about honeymoon destinations. Just think, you too can now become a bridal magazine reader.

Read The Fine Print

I would advise while you are doing your honeymoon research that you don't let the guys see you reading *Modern Bride* (consider finding a quiet corner in a closet — or even the dog house in the yard). Once you've read all of the material in the back of the magazines, there is a reader reply card that you can mail in and they will send you tons of literature on honeymoon trips. Once you've sifted through the pile with your bride-to-be, talk to a travel agent to get their input on these places. Magazines do have a tendency to over-glamorize. Don't take the printed word as "fact" (except mine, of course).

You Take The Blame

If you are selecting a "package" trip, be certain that you understand EXACTLY what the package does or does not include. Feel free to call any of the places that you are considering on their 800 number and ask a lot of questions. Get as good a feel for this place and its surroundings as possible. If you don't it will be on your head if she's miserable because of the place that "you" decided upon.

Some Unique Honeymoon Ideas

Forbes Island in the South Pacific

Manzanillo, Mexico
*stay at the Las Hadas Hotel
in the Bo Derek Suite*

A Safari in South Africa
stay at the Palace Hotel

A theatre tour of New York

Beg For The King-Size

Once you've made your decision on the location and are reserving the hotel, resort or bed and breakfast (unless you are going camping under the stars...isn't that special - NO TOILETS!) let them know that it is for your honeymoon. You're bound to get some freebies. Also, don't forget to ask for a king-sized bed if you want lots of room for honeymoon aerobics.

More Unique Honeymoon Ideas

The Grand Palazzo Hotel in St. Thomas

Swim with the dolphins at the Hilton Waikoloa Village in Hawaii

Heron Island in Australia

A South Pacific Cruise on the Windstar

A train wine tour from San Francisco to Napa Valley California

Plan To Be A Big Spender

When booking your airline reservation (unless you're driving) make destination transportation arrangements at the same time. Be certain to book your bride's preferred seating on the plane as well.

Men, be financially prepared well in advance for your honeymoon.

• Determine your budget for airlines, transportation, accommodations, meals, entertainment, long distance calls to her mother and her shopping spree(s);

• Always carry extra money (travelers checks) in case of an emergency (she may have to call her mother twice in a day);

• For the pièce-de-résistance, have a fresh bouquet of her favorite flowers waiting for her at your destination, lots of candles for the evening, chilled champagne and bring music, soft romantic music to add the final touch for having a perfect honeymoon.

Chapter 13

The Big Day

(Rivaled Only By The President's Inaugural Ball)

Cold Feet Dead Meat

THE BIG DAY...

Let's discuss "The Wedding Day" so you have all of your bases covered.

If you start to get cold feet —

GET OVER IT!

IT'S TOO LATE,
SHE'LL SEND HER MOTHER AFTER YOU!

Just The Way You Are

Marriage is a great institution guys (I wonder why they call it an institution?) You don't have to turn into Ward Cleaver. She loves you just the way you are. All the stress of planning the wedding is almost over and things will return to normal, I promise. This truly is a great day, so enjoy it.

**Treat Yourself
Before the "Big Day" With:**

A Massage

•

A Manicure (no, this will not "de-macho" you)

•

A Round of Golf with the Guys

Rings and Things

In the morning be certain that you have the final payment ready to give to the best man for the officiant, as well as the rings and the marriage license. (Tell him you will send "her mother" after him if he loses or forgets anything.) Be sure to get to the ceremony location with all of your attendants at the specified time for the photographer to begin.

Mr. and Mrs.

During the ceremony, don't worry if you forget a line or turn the wrong way. All that really matters is that you show up and end up as Mr. and Mrs.

Practice saying

"I am so glad that you are my wife"
if practiced long enough
you will probably say it in your sleep.
(Blue Ribbon for that one guys!)

Regarding Marriage

If You Look At It This Way:

You will never have to clean your own toilet.

▶ The maid will.

You will never cut your face shaving again from a new razor blade.

▶ Your blade will be nice and dull when she's finished shaving her armpits, legs and bikini line.

You will never have to drink orange juice or milk directly out of the carton again.

▶ You will be commanded to pour it in a glass.

You will no longer have to sit by yourself on New Year's Day watching football games all day.

▶ You can take advantage of all the New Year's Day sales at all of the malls with your wife.

Chapter 14

Traditional Formalities
(Don't Mess Up Now)

Smile, Shake Hands & Hug

There are a few traditional formalities you will need to get through, but these too shall pass.

• If you are having a receiving line, all you need to be is charming. Smile, shake hands and hug whenever necessary. Don't worry about remembering everyone's name, chances are that the next time you see them will be at a funeral or "another" family wedding where all you have to do is smile, shake hands and hug whenever necessary. The important names like her immediate family I guarantee her mother will never let you forget.

• Next will be the grand entrance where you and your bride are introduced at the reception to all of the guests. Enter the room without a drink in your hand and stand wherever the bandleader or DJ directs you.

Best Chance To Chug A Few

• After that will be the toast made by the best man. (You'll like this because now you can drink.) At this time her maid of honor or her father may make a toast to the new Mr. and Mrs. as well. The more people that make toasts at this time, the more you will get to drink without being yelled at.

Unacceptable Drink for the toast

- Kamikaze
- A Shot of Tequila
- Jack Daniels Straight Up

First Or Last Dance

• The next traditional event will be the first dance and the parents' dance which we have discussed at length so there is no chance that you will mess it up, unless you have already polished off a fifth of Jack Daniels to calm down. If you have, check the room for a good divorce attorney — you'll need one!

• Later in the evening will be the traditional cutting of the wedding cake and the feeding of it to each other. If at this time the mere trace of a thought of smashing the cake in your bride's face enters your mind –

ERASE IT IMMEDIATELY.

I don't care if she picks up an entire 16" layer of cake and throws it in your face. *Do not, under any circumstances retaliate.* If you ruin any part of her make-up that she spent $125.00 for and three hours of her day having professionally applied, or get even a smidgen of icing on her $2,000 wedding gown that she will never wear again–

you're dead meat!

Girls Will Be Girls

• The next event will be the throwing of the bridal bouquet where all of the single women will stand in a semi-circle behind the bride giggling, pushing and shoving each other as well as stepping on feet, if necessary, to catch the bouquet. (The one who catches the bouquet, it is said, will be the next to marry.) All you need to do at this point is watch. Pretend you're at a wrestling match and keep your eye out for a doctor in case of injury to any of the women (its been known to happen). You'd think the bride was throwing a single, naked man the way we girls carry on.

And... Boys Will Be Boys

• Finally, you will get to take the garter off your bride's leg to the tune of "The Stripper" and fling it to one of the single guys. You may take the garter off with your hands, your teeth or your tongue once you get under the 17 slips she has on under the wedding gown. All of the single men will be pushing and shoving to get a peek at what's under all of those slips as you remove the garter. However, unlike the women, once you remove the garter and are ready to fling it, the only pushing and shoving that will be going on will be to get as far away from the flying garter as possible. (Poor things — they just don't get it.)

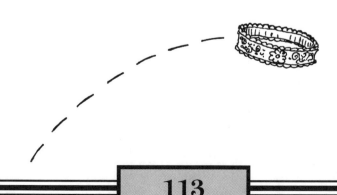

End Of A Long Day

… and that, men,
is the end of your wedding day responsibilities.

Here's to your health and happiness.

Chapter 15

Romantic Life Saving Tips

(In Case You Screwed Up Anywhere Along The Way)

Get Out Of A Jam

In case you have messed up anywhere along the line, the next several pages are dedicated to getting you out of a jam. They are 25 wonderfully romantic concepts that you can do to have her follow you anywhere...or forgive you for anything.

Key To A Happy Woman

Men, aren't you tired of being "dissed" all of the time by your significant other? "He doesn't have a romantic bone in his body," or "His idea of romance is a quickie on the kitchen table."

Well once again, I'm here to save you! If you can understand that the key to a happy woman is romance, then you've gotten yourself the brass ring. Heck, you've gotten the whole darn merry-go-round!

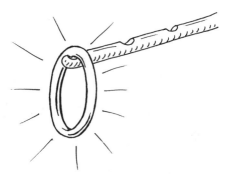

Let Her Know You Care

It is important for you guys to keep a portion of your brain reserved for romance — anytime or anywhere. You don't have to make this a science project. You just have to be thoughtful, creative and uninhibited. And guys, you'll love this, you can be selfish too, because you will benefit from becoming the *Maestro of Romance*. There is a payback - love, adoration, respect and more times than not, sex! You must understand, however, that acts of romance have no ulterior motive. Acts of romance let her know you care.

The Art Of The Deal

Remember Donald Trump's book *The Art Of The Deal*? Well romance is also an art with attitude. It's not what you do but how you do it. Auntie Mame said, "Romance is a banquet and most damned fools are starving!"

So to keep you from starving here are 25 simple, creative ideas to keep you out of hot water during this wedding planning time and for the days, weeks, months and years ahead. Every week, think of one more romantic idea, add it to the list, and try it out. You are destined for happiness – Guaranteed!

Give Her A "Bare" Hug

1. Send a stuffed teddy bear and a silk teddy that you bought at Victoria's Secret to her workplace with a note that says, "I have a "bare" hug waiting at home for you tonight."

2. Have a trophy made up that says, "World's Greatest Friend and Lover" and set it on her nightstand.

3. Arrive home from work before she does. Run a warm, scented bubble bath surrounded by candles and a glass of wine. On the front door leave her a note that says: My very special (her name), this is your time to relax. I've gone out to pick up dinner. Will see you soon. I love you (your name). (Men, you may want to pick up something that doesn't need to be eaten hot – I have a feeling this will be a very late dinner.) When you get home, dry her off with a warm towel.

4. Make a date with your significant other (there is always excitement and fun that comes with the anticipation of the evening ahead). Bring her flowers, take her out for a "special" dinner. Flirt with her across the table, hold her hand and when you get home - make love to her on a bed that has been covered with rose petals.

5. Get tickets to a play or concert that she's been dying to see and have a limo take you in style.

6. Give each other an assignment. You must each write in 75 words or less why the other is so sexy to you. You must read them in bed to each other on Wednesday night by candlelight.

Give Her A Massage

7. Surprise her with a weekend getaway to either a remote cabin with a fireplace or a quaint bed and breakfast. It doesn't have to be extravagant and you don't have to leave the state. You just need to spend time together away from wedding plans and telephones. Take long walks, have picnic lunches and remind her how important she is to you.

8. Have a romantic candlelight picnic anywhere under the stars. The ambiance surrounding the food is what's important. Feed her chocolate dipped strawberries for dessert.

9. Give her a massage. Massage her hands, her feet, her face, her back and her neck. Take your time. Let her relax. Use warm scented lotion or oil. Play soft music and surround yourselves with candles. Expect nothing for yourself but the pleasure of relaxing her.

Watch Movies In Bed

10. Grab a bottle of your favorite wine and go and watch the perfect sunset.

11. Watch movies in bed on a rainy day, order food in, and snuggle all day long.

12. Send flowers to her place of work for no particular reason. Attach a card that says, "Just thinking about you. Love, _____."

13. Bring home the puppy or the kitten she's always wanted in a basket.

Send Her A Love Song

14. Call her favorite radio station that she listens to on her way to work and dedicate a song to her.

15. Send her a card whether funny, serious or risqué to her place of business once a week on different days.

16. Do something with her that you wouldn't ordinarily do (and don't complain). You could go grocery shopping or you could take her to a romantic movie, or go to the mall.

Fulfill Her
#1 Fantasy

17. Go to The Body Shop or any bath shop and have a bath gift basket made up for her. Attach a card that says, "This is to be used for your relaxation the day before the wedding. I'll meet you at the altar. Love, _____."

18. Do one of her household chores.

19. Ask her what her number one fantasy is — and fulfill it. (She will then ask you for yours, of course, and you'll be a happy man!)

Love Slave For a Day

20. Make an assignment: Both of you must make up a book of redeemable romantic love coupons for each other, that can be spontaneously redeemed (or with some planning). Examples would be:

- A massage
- A night on the town
- I'll cook your favorite meal
- A weekend in the mountains or at the beach
- Making love in an unusual place
- A surprise present once a week for a month
- A movie
- Love slave for a day
- Good for 5 **very** romantic kisses

Anyway, you get the picture, and you both win.

21. Kiss her and hug her every day before you go to work.

What You Give Is What You Get

22. Write her a love letter and mail it to her place of business.

23. Don't roll over and go to sleep after you make love. Hold her, talk to her, ask her if you can get her anything. That sleepy state that you men get in (it's a chemical thing) will pass. Understand her needs and she will understand yours.

24. Frame her favorite picture of the two of you and send it to her place of work.

25. Treat her as your lover first - and then, cherish her as your wife.

Always remember men that what you give out you get back and as Pierre Corneille said, "The manner of giving is worth more than the gift."

About the Author

Take one hip "Dear Abby" and mix well with an uncomplicated Martha Stewart and you've got Maureen Moss, founder and owner of Constant Concepts and Maureen Moss' Fairytale Weddings.

For almost a decade, Maureen Moss has proven to hundreds of brides-and-grooms-to-be, and couples seeking the romance they once knew, that fairytales can indeed come true. Known to her clients as the "Diva of Weddings and Romance," Ms. Moss has orchestrated more than 1100 weddings around the nation and in Canada...conducts seminars on "How To Plan The Perfect Wedding" and "The Art of Romance"...and written and produced video and audio cassettes on weddings and romance for international distribution.

Residing in Phoenix, Arizona, Ms. Moss has been recognized by the media for her dramatic and creative approach to planning weddings and teaching others how to "keep romance alive." A frequent guest on talk and news shows, Ms. Moss also co-hosted a 60-minute radio show called "Love Is On The Line." Today, her wedding consultation firm is the largest in the Southwest and a growing factor across the nation. Her romance seminars continue to draw large audiences of men and women of all ages.

Maureen Moss is currently completing a companion book, entitled "Survival Guide For The Bride To Be...Or How To Avoid PWS (Pre-Wedding Syndrome)."